PHYLLIS J. LE P

CARING
—FOR—
PEOPLE
GRIEF
IN

*9 Studies for Groups
or Individuals*
With Notes for Leaders

CARING PEOPLE BIBLE STUDIES

INTERVARSITY PRESS
DOWNERS GROVE, ILLINOIS, USA
LEICESTER, ENGLAND

InterVarsity Press, USA, is the book-publishing division of InterVarsity Christian Fellowship, a student movement active on campus at hundreds of universities, colleges and schools of nursing in the United States of America, and a member movement of the International Fellowship of Evangelical Students. For information about local and regional activities, write Public Relations Dept., InterVarsity Christian Fellowship, 6400 Schroeder Rd., P.O. Box 7895, Madison, WI 53707-7895.

Inter-Varsity Press, UK, is the book-publishing division of the Universities and Colleges Christian Fellowship (formerly the Inter-Varsity Fellowship), a student movement linking Christian Unions in universities and colleges throughout the United Kingdom and the Republic of Ireland, and a member movement of the International Fellowship of Evangelical Students. For information about local and national activities write to UCCF, 38 De Montfort Street, Leicester LE1 7GP.

Some of the studies in this guide are adapted from studies written by Nurses Christian Fellowship staff.

All Scripture quotations, unless otherwise indicated, are from the Holy Bible, New International Version. Copyright © 1973, 1978, International Bible Society. Used by permission of Zondervan Bible Publishers. Published in Great Britain by Hodder and Stoughton Ltd.

Cover photograph: Michael Goss

USA ISBN 0-8308-1193-1
UK ISBN 0-85111-332-X

Printed in the United States of America

15	14	13	12	11	10	9	8	7	6	5	4	3	2	1
03	02	01	00	99	98	97	96	95	94	93	92	91		

Getting the Most from Caring People Bible Studies _____ 5

Introducing Caring for People in Grief _____ 9

1. Facing Your Own Death *Psalm 90* _____ 13

2. Overcoming the Fear of Death *Hebrews 2:9-18* _____ 16

3. Offering Comfort *John 11:17-44* _____ 20

4. Offering Peace *John 14:1-7* _____ 23

5. Offering Hope *Revelation 21:1-27* _____ 27

6. Offering Grace *2 Corinthians 4:7—5:8* _____ 30

7. Saying Goodbye to an Elderly Friend
Genesis 48:1-12; 49:22—50:14 _____ 33

8. Dealing with a Child's Death *2 Samuel 12:15-23* _____ 36

9. The Gift of Good Grief *1 Thessalonians 4:13-18* _____ 39

Leader's Notes _____ 43

Getting the Most from Caring People Bible Studies

Caring People Bible Studies are designed to show how God equips us to help others who are in need. They reveal what the Bible has to say about the pain we will all face in life and what we can do to care for friends, family, neighbors and even strangers who experience pain.

The passages you will study will be thought-provoking, challenging, inspiring and practical. They will show you how to focus on others, but they will also help you focus on yourself. Why? Because these guides are not designed merely to convince you of the truthfulness of some idea. Rather, they are intended to allow biblical truths to renew your heart and mind.

These Bible studies are inductive rather than deductive. In other words, the author will lead us to discover what the Bible says about a particular topic through a series of questions rather than simply telling us what she believes. Therefore, the studies are thought-provoking. They help us to think about the meaning of the passage so that we can truly understand what the biblical writer intended to say.

Additionally, these studies are personal. At the end of each study, you'll be given an opportunity to make a commitment to respond. And you will find guidance for prayer as well. Finally, these studies are versatile. They are designed for student, professional, neighborhood and/or church groups. They are also effective for individual study.

How They're Put Together
Caring People Bible Studies have a distinctive format. Each study takes about forty-five minutes in a group setting or thirty minutes in personal

study—unless you choose to take more time. The guides have a workbook format with space for writing responses to each question. This is ideal for personal study and allows group members to prepare in advance for the discussion. At the end of the guides are some notes for leaders. They describe how to lead a group discussion, give helpful tips on group dynamics, suggest ways to deal with problems which may arise during the discussion, and provide additional background information on certain questions. With such helps, someone with little or no experience can lead an effective study.

Suggestions for Individual Study

1. As you begin the study, pray that God will help you understand and apply the passages to your life. Pray that he will show you what kinds of action he would have you take as a result of your time of study.

2. In your first session take time to read the introduction to the entire study. This will orient you to the subject at hand and the author's goals for the studies.

3. Read the short introduction to the study.

4. Read and reread the suggested Bible passage to familiarize yourself with it.

5. A good modern translation of the Bible, rather than the King James Version or a paraphrase, will give you the most help. The New International Version, the New American Standard Bible and the Revised Standard Version are all recommended. However, the questions in this guide are based on the New International Version.

6. Use the space provided to respond to the questions. This will help you express your understanding of the passage clearly.

7. It might be good to have a Bible dictionary handy. Use it to look up any unfamiliar words, names or places.

8. Take time with the final question in each study to commit yourself to action and/or a change in attitude.

Suggestions for Group Study

1. Come to the study prepared. Follow the suggestions for individual study mentioned above. You will find that careful preparation will greatly enrich your time spent in group discussion.

2. Be willing to participate in the discussion. The leader of your group will not be lecturing. Instead, he or she will be encouraging the members of the group to discuss what they have learned. The leader will be asking the questions that are found in this guide.

3. Stick to the topic being discussed. Your answers should be based on the verses which are the focus of the discussion and not on outside authorities such as commentaries or speakers.

4. Be sensitive to the other members of the group. Listen attentively when they describe what they have learned. You may be surprised by their insights! When possible, link what you say to the comments of others. Also, be affirming whenever you can. This will encourage some of the more hesitant members of the group to participate.

5. Be careful not to dominate the discussion. We are sometimes so eager to express our thoughts that we leave too little opportunity for others to respond. By all means participate! But allow others to also.

6. Expect God to teach you through the passage being discussed and through the other members of the group. Pray that you will have an enjoyable and profitable time together, but also that as a result of the study, you will find ways that you can take action individually and/or as a group.

7. We recommend that groups follow a few basic guidelines, and that these guidelines be read at the beginning of the first session. The guidelines, which you may wish to adapt to your situation, are:

☐ Anything said in the group is considered confidential and will not be discussed outside the group unless specific permission is given to do so.

☐ We will provide time for each person present to talk if he or she feels comfortable doing so.

☐ We will talk about ourselves and our own situations, avoiding conversation about other people.

☐ We will listen attentively to each other.

☐ We will be very cautious about giving advice.

☐ We will pray for each other.

8. If you are the group leader, you will find additional suggestions at the back of the guide.

Introducing Caring for People in Grief

We were not created to die. We were created to live. When I remember that death is not a part of God's original plan I begin to understand why death is so hard to face. God did not intend for me to die. With a little help from the devil, humanity brought death on themselves.

Three of our four parents are dead. George, Lela, Judy, Stephen, Joe and Stuart have also died during the sixteen years of our marriage. These are people of all ages and significance in our lives. Some deaths were sudden and unexpected. Some were slow, a bit more predictable, and even welcomed in ways. In addition, we have grieved for many more as we have suffered with friends for those they have lost.

The vivid memories come back as I work on this study guide. I remember getting the call at one in the morning. My dad had died. Sometimes the reality of painful news takes a while to sink into my heart and emotions. Not so with my dad's death. We had expected it for months, so I could not deny its reality.

Andy's dad died less than forty-eight hours after our first child was born. We crashed rapidly from the thrill of birth to the loss of a wonderful father. Andy went alone to his dad's funeral.

Andy's mother was a vibrant and youthful seventy-two-year-old woman. During the last couple of years of her life vague symptoms hinted that she was not feeling well. She saw a doctor, was diagnosed and scheduled for surgery. We all anticipated that this would bring back her health and vitality. Instead, it took her life.

And then there was George. He not only led Andy to the Lord but faithfully discipled him and influenced him in many godly ways. At fifty, George entered seminary with the goal of being ordained and being in the ministry full-time. Soon afterward he was diagnosed with a terminal illness. At a point when chemotherapy was doing no good, he said to Andy, "It is wonderful being totally in the hands of God."

He fought the disease. He graduated from seminary. His ordination caused great celebration! Friends and family gathered from all over for the event. The pastor giving the homily said: "George, we don't know if you will be around for twenty minutes or twenty years. But that really doesn't matter. What matters is God's will and life being lived out in you." Weeks later, George died.

I remember another occasion when Andy came home from work and said gently, "I have news that is going to be very difficult for you." Stephen Brown, days before his second birthday, had drowned. As Stephen's father later said, "This was a death that came eighty years too soon."

Lela had been a wonderful roommate to me for the three years before I got married. In fact she was involved with our whole courtship. She shared our excitement, helped plan our wedding and sang at it. After our marriage, she continued to be a great friend to our family. She became "Aunty" Lela to our children. We got to the point that we thought we could do no redecorating without her. Illness and death took her from us prematurely.

Each of these persons, now missing from our world, has a story. Each made contributions to our lives. Each was painful to lose. There is still unfinished grieving in me because of these losses. Each person's death reminds me of the shortness of my own life here on earth. But there is something else that their deaths signify to me. There is something else that I share with those who know Jesus and have died before me. We will all meet again at the wedding supper of the Lamb!

"Hallelujah!
      For our Lord God Almighty reigns.
   Let us rejoice and be glad
      And give him glory!
   For the wedding of the Lamb has come,
      and his bride has made herself ready.
   Fine linen, bright and clean,
      was given her to wear." . . .

Then the angel said to me, Write:
'Blessed are those who are invited to the
wedding supper of the Lamb!' "
(Revelation 19:6-9)

One of the occasions in life that deeply satisfies me is an unhurried meal with dear friends: a time filled with the best kind of humor, a time of getting to know the other people intimately, a time of sharing struggles, of talking about how God has made a difference in our current lives, a time of worshipping him and praying together.

At best, what I have experienced of this intimacy here on earth is merely a taste of relationships in heaven. The anticipation of what it will be like gives meaning and a sense of purpose to what it is like here. Even the awful pain of death is a reminder that life is not over yet, that this is only the beginning.

The more I look at death's ugly face, and the more I confront my own mortality, the more I will know how to help others who are in pain because of death. And the more I will know how to live.

I am not alone in this. If you have not lost someone who is important to you, you will. If you have not been called upon to care for someone who is facing death, you will. The question is not "if" but "when."

Our Christian faith does not offer an easy escape from the pain of death. God does not suggest that we look the other way and avoid the tragedy of it at all costs. He doesn't even want us to act like it doesn't hurt. Jesus cried as he faced the death of his friend Lazarus. Jesus sweat drops of blood as he faced his own death.

Because of Christ's death and resurrection, though we cannot escape death, we can overcome the fear of it. We are freed from the bondage of death. We are able to look our own death squarely in the eye and declare with confidence that death has not won the victory. It is the last enemy to be destroyed. But death *will* be destroyed!

Jesus lives and so shall I.
Death! thy sting is gone forever,
He who deigned for me to die,

Lives the bands of death to sever.
He shall raise me with the just;
Jesus is my Hope and Trust.

Jesus lives, I know full well,
Naught from Him my heart can sever,
Life nor death nor pow'rs of hell,
Joy nor grief henceforth forever.
None of all his saints is lost;
Jesus is my Hope and Trust.

Jesus lives, and death is now
But my entrance into glory.
Courage then, my soul, for thou
Hast a crown of life before thee;
Thou shall find thy hopes were just;
Jesus is the Christian's Trust.
        —"Jesus Lives and So Shall I"

Jesus offers us hope, peace, comfort and grace as we face our own death. We can also offer these gifts as we walk through death with others. God has told us that yes, we need to grieve, but not like those who are without hope. In Scripture he has given us models of those who have lost their children, and of elderly people who have died with dignity because of God in their lives. And finally he has shown that, when Christ is the center of our lives, it really doesn't make a lot of difference whether we live or die. It does make a difference that we glorify God in either.

This Bible study guide is for people who are willing to face grief in their own lives—and in the lives of others. Although these studies focus on death, there are many other losses in our lives that cause us to grieve, and the principles here relate to those losses as well. My prayer for you, as you look at what Scripture says about death, is that you will be better able to care for others who are grieving.

1/Facing Your Own Death

Psalm 90

I always thought that I was going to die young. When I told my friend Rita about these thoughts, she said, "Phyllis, it's too late!"

Even though I must now admit that I am too old to die young, I was never too young to think about dying. Is thinking about death a bit unhealthy? Wasn't I being morbid? No. Facing my own death was one of the healthiest things I could do. Before I can learn to live right, I need to learn to die. And before I can help others face death, I must first learn to face my own.

1. What comes to your mind when you think about dying?

2. Read Psalm 90. Most of this psalm is about death. Why are verses 1-2 so important in setting the stage for this discussion?

3. What is life like according to verses 3-10?

4. In what ways does the psalmist express your feelings about God and life and death?

How are your attitudes different?

5. In verse 12 the psalmist makes a request of God. What do you think it means to "number our days"?

6. What is a "heart of wisdom"?

7. How does the knowledge that you are going to die affect the way you live your life?

8. Verses 11-12 stand between two contrasting sections. How do verses 3-10 differ from verses 13-17?

9. What does the psalmist ask God to do in verses 13-17?

10. How do each of these requests demonstrate a "heart of wisdom"?

11. These verses turn the focus back on God. How does this change of focus put death into perspective?

12. Why can you more effectively care for someone who is facing death if you have looked at your own death?

It has been said, "In learning to die, I learn how to live." This seems to have happened to the writer of this psalm. Ask God to make your life fuller and richer as you seek to look at your death. Ask him to be your focus whenever your life touches someone who is facing death.

2/Overcoming the Fear of Death
Hebrews 2:9-18

C. *S. Lewis wrote that he was surprised how much grief felt like fear. We live constantly with the fear of death. When death does occur (or any loss—because loss reminds us of that ultimate loss in death) the feelings of grief come to the surface and magnify the fear that has been there all along. But the Bible teaches us that we can be freed from the bondage of this fear.*

1. What are you like when you are afraid—in your behavior, in your attitudes, in your perspective, and in your body (physically)?

2. Read Hebrews 2:9-18. In verses 9-13 what do we learn about Jesus?

What is his relationship with his people?

---

3. How do you respond to being in the same family with Jesus, to being his brother or sister?

---

4. What are the effects of Jesus becoming human and dying (vv. 14-18)?

---

5. Verse 15 says that one of Christ's purposes is to "free those who all their lives were held in slavery by their fear of death." Why do people fear death?

---

6. How do you see people expressing enslavement to this fear of death?

How does the lack of freedom in talking about death reflect this bondage?

7. Why is it vital that Jesus became like his human brothers and sisters (vv. 17-18)?

8. What do you think is the relationship between the fear of meeting God and the fear of death?

9. How does the fact that Jesus made atonement for our sins speak to this fear of meeting God?

10. What difference does it make that Jesus has experienced death and has power over it?

How does this truth affect your attitudes and behavior?

11. Verse 17 says that Jesus became a merciful and faithful high priest. How can you demonstrate this mercy and faithfulness to others by helping them to identify their fears about death?

---

12. How can you communicate what this passage says about Christ and death to those who are afraid?

Pray that God will deeply touch you with this truth about his Son, that God will begin the process of relieving you from the fear of death. Ask him to use you in the lives of others who are enslaved by a fear of death.

3/Offering Comfort
John 11:17-44

The Sunday-school lesson was about Jesus raising Lazarus from the dead. Jill was abrupt, typically honest, and refreshing. "It isn't fair," she said. "When my friend dies, I have to deal with it. When Jesus' friend dies, he just raises him from the dead!"

Though Jill's feelings were legitimate, there is much more than this to John 11. Jesus is not just avoiding the sting of death by raising his friend Lazarus from the dead. We see how he related to people and experienced their sorrow as well as his own. Then we see his power over death.

1. Why does death often seem unfair?

2. Read John 11:17-44. What different emotions do you sense in this narrative?

3. In what different ways does Jesus respond to Mary's and Martha's grief?

Why doesn't he respond to Mary and Martha in the same way?

4. When you have experienced loss, what responses of people were helpful in your various stages of grief?

5. What kinds of responses were not helpful?

6. Three times, characters in this narrative say that Jesus could have prevented the death of Lazarus (see vv. 21, 32, 37). Why didn't he do it?

7. What all does Jesus say about himself in verses 25-26?

8. Jesus ended his declaration of verses 25-26 with the question "Do you believe this?" How would you answer Christ's question? Explain.

9. What effect does your answer to the above question have on the way you can give and receive comfort?

10. In verses 38-44, Jesus raises Lazarus from the dead. Why did he do this?

11. As a result of what you have learned in this passage, how can you better comfort others who are facing grief?

Pray that God will give you freedom and sensitivity as you comfort people who grieve.

4/Offering Peace

John 14:1-7

I did exactly the opposite of what the mugger told me to do. He pointed a gun at my chest, and he told me *not* to make a sound. I screamed! As a result, I thought he would kill me. The thought that flashed vividly through my mind was, "To be absent from the body is to be present with the Lord." I experienced deep peace because I expected to see Jesus. There was even a vague sense of disappointment when, instead of pulling the trigger, he hit me on the head with the other end of the gun. After grabbing my purse, he ran off.

1. Describe what it was like if you were ever near death or thought you were.

2. Read John 14:1-7. This discussion between Jesus and his disciples takes place at the last meal that they ate together before his death. They are aware that separation is coming soon. What might have surprised the disciples about Christ's instructions in verse 1?

3. The first thing that Jesus promises his disciples is that he will prepare a place for them in his father's house. If you were going to a completely new place, what difference would it make if someone you trusted were preparing for your arrival?

4. Jesus' second promise is that he will come back and take them to be with him. For some, the greatest fear of death is being alone. What it is like for you when you feel really alone?

5. In what ways can you help relieve this fear of being alone for a person who is dying? (What would you want someone to do for you?)

6. How is your anxiety about the unknown aspects of death affected by reading here that Jesus is preparing your destination and he will escort you there?

7. Finally, Jesus says that he is the way, the truth and the life. What do you think Jesus means by the terms *way, truth* and *life?*

8. How do you feel when you are driving and are lost or confused about the direction you are going in?

9. How does Jesus speak to this issue for those who are lost or uncertain about how to get to heaven?

10. What implications does Christ's statement that he is truth and life have for those who are looking for meaning, fulfillment and purpose in their lives?

11. What does it mean to *know* someone?

12. According to this passage, how can a person know God?

13. How can you offer peace to someone facing death by sharing Jesus Christ?

Pray that God will make you an instrument of his peace for those who are facing death.

5 /Offering Hope
Revelation 21:1-27

I'd expected it for weeks. Even so, when the time came, I groped for balance. "Girls. Dad is home." I have forgotten some of the words that were spoken during my father's funeral service. But those words will ring on in my heart and memory forever. "Dad is home!"

Before Daddy died, his health broke quite suddenly. Dramatic changes came. Over the months, we watched his physical deterioration. But while his body degenerated, Dad's spirit grew. He learned to know God better. He was moving closer to "home." And finally that day came when God took him to be with himself. Because Dad loved Jesus, death meant "going home" to heaven.

1. What do you hope heaven will be like?

2. Read Revelation 21:1-27. What is heaven like?

How does this description of heaven compare with what you want it to be?

_____

3. Verses 1-8 use the word *new* several times. As you think of earth as it is now, what all do you see in these verses that will be "new"?

_____

4. What difference will it make that God will finally dwell with people in this way (21:3-7, 22-23)?

_____

5. How might this kind of heaven meet some of your own deepest longings?

_____

6. How do you respond to the words "It is done. I am the Alpha and the Omega, the Beginning and the End" (v. 6)?

_____

7. How does the historical perspective seen in verses 12 and 14 add power to the words "It is done" and to the view of God as the Alpha and the Omega?

8. What do verses 22-27 further tell you about what life will be like in heaven?

9. As you think through the entire passage, how does life in heaven compare or contrast with the life that you are experiencing on earth now?

10. What aspects of life in heaven most appeal to you? Why?

11. In what different ways do you see the glory of God revealed throughout this passage?

12. How does this view of heaven affect your sense of hope?

13. How can you offer this hope to someone who is facing death?

Pray that God will enable you to be moved toward hope by the reality of heaven. Pray that you will be able to effectively share this hope with people who are facing death.

6/Offering Grace

2 Corinthians 4:7—5:8

My friend Judy died last month. I did not expect her to die. Certainly, leukemia had waged war against her body for three years. But even though I knew that her heart was failing because of the adverse affects of chemotherapy, I did not expect her to die.

She was so full of life! And that life grew dramatically as she fought for it. But it wasn't just an abundant physical life; her spiritual vitality grew as well. The abundance of the life that God gave her made her death seem unimaginable.

Yet it was the health of that life that also made her death rich. The secret was the grace of God, a grace similar to that described by the apostle Paul in a letter he wrote to new Christians in the ancient city of Corinth. When Judy's husband found her Bible shortly after her death, it was opened to 2 Corinthians 4 and 5. She had marked verses 4:7 through 5:8.

1. What is grace? (Describe, illustrate and define it as clearly as you can.)

2. Read 2 Corinthians 4:7—5:8. Though the word *grace* is used only once, what evidence is there of God's grace throughout this passage?

---

3. What is the "treasure" mentioned in 4:7? (See also 4:6.)

---

4. What are the jars of clay that Paul mentions?

---

5. How is the grace of God demonstrated by this treasure being placed in jars of clay?

---

6. How does the death of Jesus we carry in our bodies reveal the life of Jesus in us (4:8-12)?

---

7. How is the grace of God experienced through the hope of the resurrection (4:13-15)?

8. How do you see the grace of God that results from the hope of the resurrection being demonstrated in Paul's life (4:15—5:8)?

9. Compare your attitude toward illness, aging and death with Paul's view of his difficulties.

10. In what ways would you like to reflect more of God's grace in your life?

11. What steps do you need to take in order for this to happen?

12. How can you offer grace to someone who is facing death?

Pray that God's strength and grace will be working fully in you and in those to whom you minister.

7/Saying Goodbye to an Elderly Friend
Genesis 48:1-12; 49:22—50:14

A *friend wrote the following letter to God:*

"Lord, my favorite person in the whole world died last night. Thank you for the privilege of being there. It was such an honor to watch a hero leave this world and make his triumphal entry into heaven. The peace and beauty that surrounded all of us was a special blessing. Jesus' presence could be felt as he took Grandpa's hand and led him to the light. It was so precious to watch Grandma say good-by. Just before everyone came in, Grandma was standing over the bed telling Grandpa she loved him and that it was O.K. to go. We stood around his bed loving him more than could be imagined. Each one of us was able to tell him one last time 'I love you, Grandpa.' The last hug I gave him will be treasured for eternity. He looked around at each of us and then shut his loving eyes.

"His death was precious to us. The tears and sobs were felt as deeply in our hearts as they could possibly go. The tears may lessen as time goes on, but not the place in my heart that Grandpa filled up. Lord, I will always thank you for my favorite person in heaven."

1. What are common attitudes toward the elderly today?

2. Read Genesis 48:1-12; 49:22—50:14. How did Jacob respond to his impending death?

_____

3. What things were uppermost in his mind as he prepared to die?

Why do you think these things were important to him?

_____

4. What are ways that you can assist elderly people in your life to complete what is important to them?

_____

5. How did Jacob's relationship with God affect the way he faced death?

_____

6. What evidence do you see that the past was important to Jacob?

7. How might you free your own elderly friends and relatives to talk about their pasts?

8. What attitudes did Joseph demonstrate toward Jacob?

9. What was the value of Joseph bringing his children to see Jacob prior to his death?

10. Compare the attitude of Joseph toward Jacob with attitudes commonly expressed today toward elderly people.

11. In order to effectively care for the elderly who are facing death we need to know how to age and die with dignity ourselves. What changes do you need to make in your life now in order to be able to face death like Jacob did?

Pray that God will enable you to better care for elderly people in your life and that he will help you to age and face death graciously.

8/Dealing with a Child's Death
2 Samuel 12:15-23

I was doing dishes with my mother-in-law one evening. I began asking her questions about Lucy Rae, her daughter who had died at age seven some thirty years before. Lucy Rae had been ill with polio less than twenty-four hours before her death. Mom's blue eyes filled with tears as she spoke. Though it did not surface often, the pain was still deep within her being.

There is some pain that you never "get over." Time lessens the intensity of it. God's love and grace heal. But it is never completely gone, at least not this side of heaven. I believe that is the way it is when you lose a child in death.

1. How do you think you would respond if your child were diagnosed with a terminal illness?

2. Read 2 Samuel 12:15-23. Describe David's attitudes and behavior before the death of his child.

3. What similar responses have you seen or heard of in the parents of a child who was dying?

---

4. How might your response be like David's if your own child were critically ill?

---

5. Why do you think the elders behaved the way they did?

---

6. How free do you think you would be to allow someone to express overwhelming grief?

---

7. How might you effectively support someone who is in the process of losing a child?

---

8. In what ways did David's servants and elders fail to understand his grief?

9. How do their actions reflect some of your own fears of relating to parents of a child who has died?

10. What kinds of responses might be helpful when relating to parents after their child has died?

11. David's behavior changed dramatically after the death of his son. Why did he respond in this way?

12. What comfort did David have in the child's death (v. 23)?

13. How can you know this comfort personally?

How can you share it with others?

Pray that God will give you wisdom, courage and strength to minister to parents facing the death (or loss in other ways) of their child.

9/The Gift of Good Grief
1 Thessalonians 4:13-18

I used to be the kind of person who did not want to "waste" time grieving. I wanted to go on with life. I had to be reminded by a friend to let myself experience grief. She saw my grief coming out in other forms, less healthy ways. She also reminded me that, if I took shortcuts in the grieving process, I would expect this of others as well. My ministry to them could be hindered.

The apostle Paul coped with a similar question when he wrote to the Christians in Thessalonica. Believers there had died—some as martyrs. Paul did not tell those who were left to stop grieving. But he did say that Christian grief is different. And better.

---

1. Describe grief. (What causes grief? How does grief feel? What does a grieving person do and think?)

---

2. Read 1 Thessalonians 4:13-18. If you were caught in grief, how would these words make you feel? Please explain your response.

_____

3. What words and phrases in this passage would help you believe that the events described here really will come about?

_____

4. Paul said that he did not want his readers to be "ignorant about those who have fallen asleep." What did he want us to know about them?

_____

5. Jesus Christ is mentioned eight times here. What all can we know about Jesus from these verses?

_____

6. One person experiencing grief said, "The Christian faith offers hope—and I don't see much else to hope for right now." What is there about death that diminishes hope?

_____

7. What aspects of Paul's information here can keep believers from a "grief like the rest of men who have no hope"?

8. Paul did not prohibit grief. He spoke, instead, of a grief that contains hope. Why might some Christians feel that it is wrong to express grief?

9. What problems can result from this kind of restraint? (Consider physical, emotional and spiritual results.)

10. Using the concepts in this passage, how would you describe good grief?

11. If you had a friend caught in grief, how could you offer godly hope—without denying a healthy grief process? (What specifically could you do to encourage healthy grief? What specifically could you do to offer hope?)

12. Paul ends this section of his letter with, "Therefore encourage each other with these words." If you were dying, how would this passage encourage you?

13. If you are one of those who "are left," how does this passage encourage you?

Ask God to help you give healthy expression to the grief in your own life. Pray that you will be able to walk beside those who grieve and to offer godly hope.

Leader's Notes

Leading a Bible discussion can be an enjoyable and rewarding experience. But it can also be intimidating—especially if you've never done it before. If this is how you feel, you're in good company.

When God asked Moses to lead the Israelites out of Egypt, he replied, "O Lord, please send someone else to do it!" (Ex 4:13). But God's response to all of his servants—including you—is essentially the same: "My grace is sufficient for you" (2 Cor 12:9).

There is another reason you should feel encouraged. Leading a Bible discussion is not difficult if you follow certain guidelines. You don't need to be an expert on the Bible or a trained teacher. The suggestions listed below should enable you to effectively and enjoyably fulfill your role as leader.

Using Caring People Bible Studies

Where should you begin? A good starting place is *Handbook for Caring People*. This short book helps develop some basic caring skills like listening to and communicating to people who are in pain. Additionally, it will help you understand the stages that people in grief go through and how to help people who are suffering. Most of all, this book shows how to rely on God for the strength you need to care for others. At the end of each chapter, you'll find questions for individual or group use.

For the next step you might choose *Resources for Caring People* or *The*

Character of Caring People. Resources for Caring People will show how God empowers us to serve others through Scripture, prayer, the Holy Spirit and many other gifts. *The Character of Caring People* shows what the heart of the Christian caregiver is like. The concerns which emerge within the group during the studies will provide you with guidance for what to do next. All of the guides give help and encouragement to those who want to care for others, but different groups may find some guides more useful than others.

You might want to focus on specific concerns like *Caring for People in Grief* or *Caring for People in Conflict.* Or your group might choose to study topics which reflect areas they need to grow in. For instance, those who have sick friends or relatives or who simply want to be more sensitive to the physical needs that are all around us will find *Caring for Physical Needs* helpful. Others may want to know more about the spiritual concerns people have. *Caring for Spiritual Needs* is a great resource for this. For a biblical perspective on how God wants us to deal with emotional problems, you might choose *Caring for Emotional Needs.* The key is to remember that we all have these needs. Our physical condition affects us spiritually and emotionally. A spiritual problem can have physical and emotional consequences. By covering several of these guides in sequence, members of your group will develop a complete picture of what it means to be a caring Christian.

Preparing for the Study

1. Ask God to help you understand and apply the passage in your own life. Unless this happens, you will not be prepared to lead others. Pray too for the various members of the group. Ask God to open your hearts to the message of his Word and to motivate you to action.

2. Read the introduction to the entire guide to get an overview of the subject at hand and the issues which will be explored.

3. As you begin each study, read and reread the assigned Bible passage to familiarize yourself with it.

4. This study guide is based on the New International Version of the Bible. It will help you and the group if you use this translation as the basis for your study and discussion.

5. Carefully work through each question in the study. Spend time in meditation and reflection as you consider how to respond.

6. Write your thoughts and responses in the space provided in the study guide. This will help you to express your understanding of the passage clearly.

7. It might help you to have a Bible dictionary handy. Use it to look up any unfamiliar words, names or places. (For additional help on how to study a passage, see chapter five of *Leading Bible Discussions,* IVP.)

8. Take the response portion of each study seriously. Consider what this means for your life—what changes you might need to make in your lifestyle and/or actions you need to take in the world. Remember that the group will follow your lead in responding to the studies.

Leading the Study

1. Begin the study on time. Open with prayer, asking God to help the group to understand and apply the passage.

2. Be sure that everyone in your group has a study guide. Encourage the group to prepare beforehand for each discussion by reading the introduction to the guide and by working through the questions in the study.

3. At the beginning of your first time together, explain that these studies are meant to be discussions, not lectures. Encourage the members of the group to participate. However, do not put pressure on those who may be hesitant to speak during the first few sessions.

4. Have a group member read the introductory paragraph at the beginning of the discussion. This will orient the group to the topic of the study.

5. Every study begins with an "approach" question, which is meant to be asked before the passage is read. These questions are important for several reasons.

First, there is always a stiffness that needs to be overcome before people will begin to talk openly. A good question will break the ice.

Second, most people will have lots of different things going on in their minds (dinner, an important meeting coming up, how to get the car fixed) that will have nothing to do with the study. A creative question will get their attention and draw them into the discussion.

Third, approach questions can reveal where our thoughts or feelings need to be transformed by Scripture. That is why it is especially important not to read the passage before the approach question is asked. The passage will tend to color the honest reactions people would otherwise give because they are, of course, supposed to think the way the Bible does.

6. Have a group member read aloud the passage to be studied.

7. As you ask the questions, keep in mind that they are designed to be used just as they are written. You may simply read them aloud. Or you may prefer to express them in your own words. There may be times when it is appropriate to deviate from the study guide. For example, a question may have already been answered. If so, move on to the next question. Or someone may raise an important question not covered in the guide. Take time to discuss it, but try to keep the group from going off on tangents.

8. Avoid answering your own questions. If necessary, repeat or rephrase them until they are clearly understood. An eager group quickly becomes passive and silent if they think the leader will do most of the talking.

9. Don't be afraid of silence. People may need time to think about the question before formulating their answers.

10. Don't be content with just one answer. Ask, "What do the rest of you think?" or "Anything else?" until several people have given answers to the question.

11. Acknowledge all contributions. Try to be affirming whenever possible. Never reject an answer. If it is clearly off-base, ask, "Which verse led you to that conclusion?" or again, "What do the rest of you think?"

12. Don't expect every answer to be addressed to you, even though this will probably happen at first. As group members become more at ease, they will begin to truly interact with each other. This is one sign of healthy discussion.

13. Don't be afraid of controversy. It can be very stimulating. If you don't resolve an issue completely, don't be frustrated. Move on and keep it in mind for later. A subsequent study may solve the problem.

14. Periodically summarize what the group has said about the passage. This helps to draw together the various ideas mentioned and gives continuity to the study. But don't preach.

15. Don't skip over the response questions. It's important that we not lose the focus of helping others even as we reflect on ourselves. Be willing to get things started by describing how you have been affected by the study.

16. Conclude your time together with conversational prayer. Ask for God's help in following through on the commitments you've made.

17. End on time. Many more suggestions and helps are found in *Small Group Leader's Handbook* and *Good Things Come in Small Groups* (both from IVP). Reading through one of these books would be worth your time.

Listening to Emotional Pain

Caring People Bible Studies are designed to take seriously the pain and struggle that is part of life. People will experience a variety of emotions during these studies. Keep in mind that you are not expected to act as a professional counselor. However, part of your role as group leader may be to listen to emotional pain. Listening is a gift which you can give to a person who is hurting. For many people, it is not an easy gift to give. The following suggestions will help you to listen more effectively to people in emotional pain.

1. Remember that you are not responsible to take the pain away. People in helping relationships often feel that they are being asked to make the other person feel better. This may be related to the helper not being comfortable with painful feelings.

2. Not only are you not responsible to take the pain away, one of the things people need most is an opportunity to face and to experience the pain in their lives. Many have spent years denying their pain and running from it. Healing can come when we are able to face our pain in the presence of someone who cares about us. Rather than trying to take the pain away, then, commit yourself to listening attentively as it is expressed.

3. Realize that some group members may not feel comfortable with others' expressions of sadness or anger. You may want to acknowledge that such emotions are uncomfortable, but say that learning to feel our own pain is often the first step in helping others with their pain.

4. Be very cautious about giving answers and advice. Advice and answers may make you feel better or feel competent, but they may also minimize people's problems and their painful feelings. Simple solutions rarely work, and they can easily communicate "You should be better now" or "You shouldn't really be talking about this."

5. Be sure to communicate direct affirmation any time people talk about their painful emotions. It takes courage to talk about our pain because it creates anxiety for us. It is a great gift to be trusted by those who are struggling.

The following notes refer to specific questions in the study:

Study 1. Facing Your Own Death. Psalm 90.

Purpose: To look at the reality of our own death in order to be wiser about our lives. To use awareness of our own death to better care for others who must die.

Question 1. We live in a death-denying culture. North Americans do everything they can to avoid the subject of death. It may be difficult for people to respond to this question. Be sensitive to the feelings of the individuals in the group. Be ready to share from your own experience. And be ready with follow-up questions if needed. For example: What does it feel like when you think about dying? How much do you try to avoid thinking about it?

Question 2. At the beginning of our lives there is God, who has always been. At the end of our lives there is God, who always will be. Thinking about death means thinking about God. For the Christian, it is God and his everlasting care that makes us able to endure the pain of death and to see purpose in it. This psalm begins and ends with the focus on God. It, therefore, puts death in its rightful context and makes it bearable.

Question 4. Keep in mind that at different times we are at different places in our attitudes about life and death and God. Encourage the group to talk not only about where they are but where they have been in their attitudes about life and death. Sometimes the mere reality of death can cause a feeling that "life is in vain." Some Christians consider these thoughts unacceptable. So they avoid them. But if we cannot look honestly at feelings about our own death, it is impossible to help others to do so.

Question 5. "Human life is set between two points in this Psalm: the wrath of God, which makes life transient, and peace with God, which gives it stability and permanency. The concluding prayer asks for the latter experience.

"It starts with verse 12 by asking for a change of attitude: first, on man's part, that, taught by God, he may learn wisdom in his brief life; and secondly, on God's part, that He might turn from His just wrath to tender pity" (*The New*

Bible Commentary: Revised [Eerdmans: Grand Rapids, Mich.: 1973], pp. 508).

Your group should come to definitions similar to these:

To "number our days" means a deep awareness of the shortness of life, that apart from God—life is nothing. It means making the most of this short life we have.

Question 6. A "heart of wisdom" is seeing life from God's perspective and living it accordingly.

Study 2. Overcoming the Fear of Death. Hebrews 2:9-18.

Purpose: To consider that Jesus became human. To experience release from the fear of death because of his death and resurrection.

Question 2. Your group should find nearly a dozen answers in these verses. Of the general thrust, one scholar says: "Our Lord's work issues on His becoming the Head of a saved company or community, i.e. those whom God has given Him through and because of what he has done. The Old Testament quotations used to confirm this are remarkable. The first is from Psalm 22 which foreshadows the cross. The second is from Isaiah 8:17-18" (*The New Bible Commentary,* pp. 1197).

Question 4. This is a profound passage. Help the group to grapple with Jesus sharing in our humanity so totally. The group should begin by observing precise answers in the passage. (Phrases such as "since," "so that," "for this reason," "because," are clues that point to effects.) Once the group has made these observations, discuss their meaning and impact in depth.

Question 5. Depending on the group you might want to move from why people fear death to "Why do you fear death?"

Question 6. This expression of fear in people might be overt and obvious. Your group should mention these first. But you should also talk about the more covert and less obvious expressions of this enslavement. For example, our whole advertising system is based on "youth," "physical beauty" and "sexual attractiveness"—as if that is what life is all about, as if we are going to live forever. Mid-life crisis is an expression of being enslaved to the fear of death. At mid-life, people worry, "Life is half over; what do I have to show for it?" The whole trend toward extramarital affairs is a statement of the fear of death. An affair says, "I still have power. I still have good life left in me."

Question 8. A follow-up question might be: How do you feel about meeting someone with whom you have an unresolved conflict?

Even atheists who verbalize no fear about meeting God will wonder at the time of their death about the possibility of being wrong.

It has been said that when people enter a hospital, death becomes a part of their thinking, whether verbalized or not—even if the cause for admission to the hospital is minor.

Question 10. Try to get beyond what the difference *should be* to what *it is* and how to fill the gap in between.

Question 11. By not being afraid to talk about death yourself, you can provide an environment in which others can share their fears about death. We must listen long and hard and accept what the people have to say. Questions that gently probe into feelings and thoughts are very helpful in helping people to identify their fears about death. Praying for and with the individual is also a comfort and help.

Question 12. There is a big difference between quoting Scripture *at* someone and sharing the message *with* someone. The first is usually with an attitude of "I've done my duty." The second is accomplished by living out the message before people. In this case, sharing the message with someone means living out the freedom from the fear of death that I am experiencing. It means demonstrating hope when that person's sense of hope is gone. It also means reading and sharing the words of Scripture and the hope that is within the Word of God at the right time. Apart from behavior that reflects those beliefs even reading Scripture can become another exercise in "quoting at."

Study 3. Offering Comfort. John 11:17-44.

Purpose: To look at the way Jesus offers comfort because of his power over death. To grow in our ability to comfort others.

Question 2. Use this question to survey the passage. Help participants to track the discussion by asking each person to name a verse or phrase that expresses each emotion.

Question 3. Note: In the event that any in the group are familiar with the grief cycle and bring it up, the following is an overview:

Denial: "It can't be!" A period of time in which the loss is completely unreal.

This stage is sometimes called *shock*. It is a protective time in which our resources have a time to gather for all that is ahead in dealing with this loss.

Anger: "It has happened! Why has this happened to me?" A period of time when the loss becomes real, and strong feelings of unfairness and antagonism may result. Some of the ways it may be demonstrated are outbursts, sobbing withdrawal or lashing out at others.

Bargaining: "God, if you will change this situation, I will. . . ." The person tries to make a deal with God.

Depression: The situation does not change. There is deep sadness and resignation as the typical signs of depression set in. This is usually the longest stage and for many the most difficult time in which to give care. Our tendency is to want people to "snap out of it."

Acceptance: The stage in which there is finally peace. The person has come to terms with the loss. This does not mean there is no sorrow—there can be deep sorrow but also deep peace in acceptance.

Question 3. Mary seems to be depressed and angry in this passage. Martha seems, on the other hand, to be looking for hope in the situation. She may even be bargaining with Jesus.

Jesus responds to Mary with deep feelings, his physical presence, weeping, and silence rather than by giving her a verbal response. Jesus responds to Martha with verbal interaction and words of hope—as well as with his presence. A similar verbal response to Mary probably would have made her more angry. Angry and depressed people want to be listened to. They do not want answers. Jesus "met them where they were."

Questions 4-5. We have all had experiences of being helped and being hurt by others when we are in pain. Looking at what helped and what was unhelpful will prepare us to more effectively comfort another person.

Question 6. Opinions may vary. Help group members to substantiate these opinions from the passage. Among other ideas, your group may observe that Christ's intimate contact with real physical death and grief helps prepare us for the same. Your group may come up with more complete answers to this question as you study verses 25 and 26 and also question 10.

Question 8. Encourage any who have been quiet, particularly any whose faith may be fuzzy, to answer this question. Listen appreciatively to any honest answers. Then move on to question 9.

Question 10. Some of the reasons are clear from what is in the passage and some as a result of speculating because of what is in the passage.

In verse 23, Jesus says that he is going to raise Lazarus. So it is simply a matter of keeping his word.

In verse 40, Jesus says it would display the glory of God.

In verse 42, so that people would know that God sent Jesus. (In verse 37 this issue is in the minds of the people.)

Jesus comforted those he loved.

Question 11. Besides reviewing how Jesus responded to people facing grief and how he is a model for our responding, help the group see the hope Christ offers and how vital this is to comforting others. Discuss how we can effectively communicate the message of this hope in Christ's power over death, his being the resurrection and the life, and what it means to believe in him.

Study 4. Offering Peace. John 14:1-7.

Purpose: To discover who Jesus Christ is and how he gives peace at the time of death.

Question 1. It is possible that no one in the group has been near death. You then may need to ask, "What do you think it would be like to be near death?"

Question 5. The fact that Jesus literally will come and take us to himself at death offers great peace to the dying Christian. His presence in this way speaks to the fear of being alone at the time of death. We also can be a source of peace and help to relieve this fear. We can be "there with" the person facing death. In my mind I envision literally holding the hand of someone who is dying until the last breath is taken—and then Jesus takes the person's hand on the other side.

I can also offer peace in preparation for that death even if I am not there at the time the person actually dies. Just allowing the person's death to be a topic of communication offers freedom and release. The natural inclination is to avoid the topic, and therefore cause the person to feel alone in the process, even if there are people around at all times.

Another aspect of meeting the aloneness of death is to remind people about the truth of Jesus. I have often said that I would want people dear to me to stay with me when I am dying. I would want to talk about my death. And I would want them to remind and assure me that all that I believe about Jesus is true.

Question 7. Help the group discuss what "way, truth and life" mean in practical terms and then what it means that Jesus is all of these—spiritually.

The way to God lies in the knowledge of the truth about him and in the experience of his life. It is precisely this knowledge and this experience which Jesus throughout His incarnate life and supremely in His atoning sacrifice, is bringing within men's reach. Jesus Himself is therefore the way, because he is the embodiment of the truth about God and His relationship with men; and by reason of this, the life that is inherent in His own words and actions, the very life of God Himself, is available for mankind. Because to know Jesus is to know the Father, the disciples in fact already have knowledge of the way to the Father. (R.V.G. Tasker, *The Gospel According to St. John,* Tyndale New Testament Commentaries [Grand Rapids, Mich.: Eerdmans, 1978], p. 165.)

Study 5. Offering Hope. Revelation 21:1-27.

Purpose: To consider that the reality of heaven and what heaven is like gives me hope. To offer that hope to those who face death.

Question 2. The description of heaven in this passage will probably far exceed what the members of your group would even dream it to be like. Thinking about heaven the way it is described here will help make it more real. Since the passage is lengthy, help the group members stay together by pointing out descriptive phrases and verse numbers as they discuss the question.

Questions 3-4. Though we know God and have had him revealed to us through Jesus Christ, the fallenness of our world and of nature prevents us from fully experiencing him. These limitations will be completely lifted in heaven. "Now the dwelling of God is with men, and he will live with them. They will be his people, and God himself will be with them and be their God." This will make a tremendous difference! Help the group to look closely at the passage, to discuss freely, and to feel this wonderful truth.

Question 5. Larry Crabb, a noted Christian psychologist, states in his film series *From the Inside Out* that there are some longings, some thirsts that will not be satisfied until we get to heaven. These longings have a lot to do with how we live life. Try to provide an environment in which people can discuss deep longings, even those that will only be completely fulfilled in heaven. As Crabb says, "The thirsts are not wrong. The problem is how we try to quench them."

Question 6. There is a sense of sureness, completion, totality in these words. It has all come together. It now makes sense. He who has always *been* in control is now *seen* to be in control. His purpose is fulfilled.

Question 7. The fact that the twelve tribes of Israel and twelve apostles are written on the gates and foundations helps paint the picture of wholeness. It is done; God's purpose throughout all of history is brought to completion.

Question 9. This question should bring to the minds, as well as the emotions, of the group members the vanity of our frequent emphasis on the now and the material. We need to see what it is really like now—compared to what it will be.

The study is not meant to bring people to the point of "being so heavenly minded that they are no earthly good." But such a weakness does not seem to be the bent in our culture. We are hardly aware of heaven! Use this question to deepen awareness of this future (and far longer) existence.

Study 6. Offering Grace. 2 Corinthians 4:7—5:8.

Purpose: To examine the grace of God as demonstrated in Paul's life. To discover how this grace gives meaning in life as well as at the time of death.

Question 1. "Unmerited favor." It is the usual thumbnail definition of grace. This definition speaks of all the good that we receive from God. It speaks of God's initiative in bringing us to himself. Your discussion will probably begin with that terse definition, but try to move the group on to a more thorough understanding of the grace concept and how the grace of God affects our daily lives. This is a wonderful passage on the grace of God lived out in Paul's life. But your group may miss its impact if you do not start out with a broad understanding of the meaning of grace.

Consider, for instance, the passage in 2 Corinthians 12:9. Here grace is defined as God's power in us, "But he said to me, 'My grace is sufficient for you, for my power is made perfect in weakness.' Therefore I will boast all the more gladly about my weaknesses, so that Christ's power may rest on me."

"Grace involves such subjects as forgiveness, salvation, regeneration, repentance, and the love of God. There are 'grace' words which do not contain the word 'grace' such as mercy, kindness, lovingkindness and goodness" (J. D. Douglas, ed., *New Bible Dictionary* [London: Inter-Varsity Press, 1963], p. 491).

Dictionary definitions range as follows: the condition or fact of being favored; mercy; divine influence acting in humanity to make them pure and morally strong.

From all of this, we can see that grace implies what God, in his power, continues to do in the lives of his people.

Some of these ideas may come automatically into your discussion. Be ready, however, to supply missing concepts before moving on to the next question.

Question 2. This question acts as an overview of the whole passage. Use it to gain a broad perspective of grace, as Paul experienced it, and as he expected to see it in the Christians at Corinth. Be careful, however, not to spend too much time. More answers will become apparent as you progress through the study.

Question 4-5. The jars of clay are the mortal bodies of believers in Jesus. The treasure is, of course, the message of Christ's Gospel, as explained in 4:6. Our bodies, like clay, are plain, ordinary, fragile. We might break. We might embarrass him. And we (our bodies) are very temporary.

Question 6. "Paul's 'dying' day after day . . . was a sharing of his Master's earthly experience as a man. This is stressed by the reiteration of the personal name *Jesus*. Through such excessive sufferings the powerful *life of Jesus* was also being more clearly revealed in him." In verse 12 "the paradox of v. 11 is repeated; Paul points out that the Corinthians reap the benefit of what he is going through" (*The New Bible Commentary*, p. 1079).

Question 7. What greater evidence is there of the grace of God in us than for us all to be raised together—even as the Lord Jesus was raised. The more people in whom this work of grace is seen the greater the cause for thanksgiving.

Question 8. Don't skimp on time here. Your group should point out nearly a dozen answers in the text.

Study 7. Saying Goodbye to an Elderly Friend. Genesis 48:1-12; 49:22—50:14.

Purpose: To examine responses of elderly persons and their families toward dying. To try to better understand how to care for the elderly person facing death.

Question 3. Although Genesis 49:22-28 is a prophetic passage, it also reveals Jacob's love for his son Joseph. He praises Joseph's good qualities. Jacob also focuses on God and what God has done for Joseph.

Question 5. In Genesis 48:1-12, Jacob remembers God's promise given to him at Luz. This promise applied to Jacob's progeny, so Jacob recounted it to his son and grandsons. Then Jacob adopted Joseph's two sons and declared that it was God who had allowed him to see the children.

In the bedside scene of Genesis 49:1-28, Jacob acted as God's prophet and also as a spokesman for God's judgment. Jacob did not always walk with God during his own lifetime. But at death, he heard God's word and spoke it to his family.

Question 6. The older one gets, the clearer the memories of the distant past become. My mother says she can remember things in her childhood like they happened yesterday—but don't ask her what she did yesterday! Jacob readily slips into talking about a very significant event in his past, the death and burial of his beloved Rachel. He also remembered events in the lives of his children—and mentioned them (along with appropriate blessing or curse) at the bedside vigil of chapter 49.

Question 7. Asking questions of older friends about their past and what is important to them is one way to free them to talk. Active listening to them is another. Just giving of your time to spend with them is telling them, "You are important and I want to know you." Affirming with words their past and its importance is freeing to them. And be patient. Older people repeat the significant stories of their lives. Their distant memories recall the events. Their close-up memories forget that they've already told you.

Question 11. It may seem strange to suddenly stop talking about the elderly and begin talking about ourselves, but we need to begin now, no matter how old we are, to learn how to age and to die. For more help in this area, I recommend Paul Tournier's *Learning to Grow Old* (Harper & Row).

Study 8. Dealing with a Child's Death. 2 Samuel 12:15-23.

Purpose: To examine and understand David's behavior and response to God before and after the death of his son. As a result of this, to begin to develop ways of comforting the families of dying children.

Question 1. Though our emphasis in this study is caring for people who are facing the death of a child, it will be good for the group to keep in mind that there are other ways of losing children besides death. The children may still be around, but you lose them emotionally. They may be lost to drugs or alcohol. They may be lost to peers, a cultic group, living with someone out of wedlock, or an unwise marriage. The pain, grief, loss is much the same. Some of the same fears that inhibit us from effectively ministering to parents with dying children also are present when we attempt to minister to parents in these other situations.

Question 3. It is likely that many in your group have not lost a child or been involved with people that have. Even so, the study is worth time and consideration—to prepare for the future.

If there are members of the group who themselves have lost a child in any way, provide an environment for them to share freely, to display their deep emotions so that the process of healing can continue—or to remain silent. You might have someone in the group who is now losing a child. If so, provide follow-up support, sensitivity and prayer.

Question 5. We live in a society that does not deal well with pain. We want to "get him up from the ground" immediately. We must learn, instead, to walk through the pain with people we care about. These questions are meant to help us walk with them. We must look at the way the elders treated David, look at our own tendencies in this area and help each other by discussing ways to avoid the "quick fix" syndrome. In this way, we can bring real help in times of need.

Questions 6-7. Fear keeps us from getting involved with people who are grieving. Because the death of a child is especially tragic, the fears are even greater. What if I say the wrong thing? What if the person falls apart? ("He may do something desperate" [v. 18].) What if I do not know what to do? What if they break up emotionally?

Help the group to discuss these fears realistically, suggest to each other ways of dealing with them, and recognize the importance of not allowing the fears to cause you to withdraw from the situation. We can remember that God is there and living his life through us. He has not left us alone in it.

Question 12. "I will go to him" means that David will join his child in heaven.

Study 9. The Gift of Good Grief. 1 Thessalonians 4:13-18.

Purpose: To understand that grief is unavoidable. To see how hope in Christ's return affects grief. To use that hope to help people who grieve.

Question 2. Look for emotional responses here. Detailed analysis will come later in the study.

Question 3. Your group should spot such phrases as "Jesus died and rose again" (v. 14), "God will bring with Jesus" (v. 14), "according to the Lord's own word" (v. 15), "for the Lord himself will come down" (v. 16). These statements are by no means proof, particularly to one who views Scripture with doubt. But they do have the ring of authenticity.

Question 5. Help your group to spot and comment on each of the eight references to Jesus. Some of this information will have emerged in previous questions. Just acknowledge any repetition and go on.

Question 6. Be sensitive here to anyone who has experienced intense grief. If the grief is not too fresh, that person may be able to express the sense of hopelessness that death brings. This will help prepare the others for a similar experience.

You may hear such answers as: "I knew I could never talk to her again. All of my hopes for a future with her vanished. The children she could have borne will never exist. I can never hope to reconcile our last argument. I don't feel as hopeful about life in general. I feel that death is lurking around the corner for everyone that I feel close to, so I feel guarded about my hopes for a future with them too. Instead of hoping for the best, I seem to expect the worst, because the worst has already happened once before."

Question 7. Paul doesn't say much that is hopeful about life here. He doesn't say, "You will feel better tomorrow." But Paul does point out that life here is not all that there is. And life here will have an abrupt and glorious end. In this, there is hope. Help your group to find specific ingredients surrounding Christ's return that would bring hope—even in the midst of grief.

If you need a follow-up question ask, "What would it be like to grieve and not have any hope?"

Questions 8-9. "Hold a stiff smile and don't cry at the funeral" is a burden that some Christians mistakenly place on themselves and each other. They think that we should prove our faith to observers by not indulging in normal grief. After all, the argument goes, we should be happy that our friend is in heaven with Jesus. Help your group to discuss this problem and its resulting damage.

Question 11. Help your group to be as specific and practical as possible here. Those who have experienced grief can be a great help to the discussion.

About the Author

Phyllis J. Le Peau is a registered nurse and a former Nurses Christian Fellowship staffworker. Currently, she is assistant program director for Wellness, Inc. Phyllis is also the author of the Fruit of the Spirit Bible Studies Kindness, Gentleness *and* Joy *(Zondervan) and coauthor of* Disciplemakers' Handbook *(IVP). With her husband, Andy, she has coauthored* One Plus One Equals One *and the LifeGuide® Bible Studies* Ephesians *and* James *(IVP/SU). She and her husband live in Downers Grove, Illinois, with their four children.*

Caring People Bible Studies from InterVarsity Press
By Phyllis J. Le Peau

Handbook for Caring People (coauthored by Bonnie J. Miller). This book provides simple, time-tested principles for dealing with the pain, the questions and the crises people face. You will get the basic tools for communication plus some practical suggestions. Questions for group discussion are at the end of each chapter.

Resources for Caring People. Through God, we have the resources we need to help others. God has given us Scripture, prayer, the Holy Spirit, listening and acceptance. This guide will show you how he works through people like you every day. 8 studies.

The Character of Caring People. The key to caring is character. These Bible studies will show you how to focus on the gifts of caring which God has given you—such as hospitality, generosity and encouragement. 8 studies.

Caring for Spiritual Needs. A relationship with God. Meaning and purpose. Belonging. Love. Assurance. These are just some of the spiritual needs that we all have. This Bible study guide will help you learn how these needs can be met in your life and in the lives of others. 9 studies.

Caring for Emotional Needs. We think we have to act like we have it all together, yet sometimes we are lonely, afraid or depressed. Christians have emotional needs just like everyone else. This Bible study guide shows how to find emotional health for ourselves and how to help others. 9 studies.

Caring for Physical Needs. When we are sick or when our basic needs for food, clothing and adequate housing are not being met, our whole being—body, spirit and emotion—is affected. When we care for the physical needs of others, we are showing God's love. These Bible studies will help you learn to do that. 8 studies.

Caring for People in Conflict. Divided churches. Broken friendships. Angry children. Torn marriages. We all have to deal with conflict and the emotions which accompany it. These studies will show you how God can bring healing and reconciliation. 9 studies.

Caring for People in Grief. Because sin brought death into the world, we all have to look into death's ugly face at one time or another. These Bible studies cover the issues which consume those who are grieving—fear, peace, grace and hope—and show you how to provide them with comfort. 9 studies.